HOLD THE LINE
TRAIL GUIDE
DAILY PRAYERS

shewill
CONFERENCE

Hold the Line Prayer Guide (Daily Prayers)

8 Owls Publishing creates books that effectively advance God's Kingdom. You may find the full list of the books we offer on our website at 8owlspublishing.com.

Copyright © 2024
First Edition
Cover Design: Kellen Catlin and Shelsea Becker

Please note that 8 Owls Publishing uses capitalization when referencing God and/or other Kingdom terminology that may differ from other publishers or grammatical trends. 8 Owls Publishing uses the English Standard Version of the Bible, published by Crossway in Wheaton, Illinois, unless otherwise noted.

ESV: Study Bible: English Standard Version. Wheaton, Ill: Crossway Bibles, 2007. Print.

Hey there, Trailblazer!

Jeremiah 29:12-13 (NIV) says, "Then you will call on Me and come and pray to Me, and I will listen to you. You will seek Me and find Me when you seek Me with all your heart."

Did you know the Lord not only hears you, but wants to hear from you? He desires a deep, meaningful relationship with you, just as He walked and talked with Adam and Eve in the Garden of Eden. Imagine that—intimate conversations with the Creator! Like any relationship, knowing Him requires time, attention, and a sincere heart. I want to know my Redeemer, and I believe you do too.

Prayer is more than words; it's a posture of the heart. It's personal, it's vital, and it's the foundation of a close relationship with God. The Bible tells us much about prayer—there are 650 prayers recorded in its pages, with approximately 450 of them answered. The first mention of prayer is in Genesis 4:26, marking a shift where people began to call upon the Lord (unlike earlier dialogues initiated directly by God, as seen in Genesis 3:8-13 and Genesis 4:9.) Throughout His earthly ministry, Jesus prayed 25 different times, showing us the importance of prayer in our lives. Additionally, the Apostle Paul emphasizes the importance of prayer 41 times in his letters, encouraging us to pray, make requests, and communicate openly with God.

My prayer is that this book and journal serve as a practical tool for you whenever you need it. Whether it's in your pocket, purse, or glove box, let this be your go-to guide on all things prayer. Our team has answered many of the common questions surrounding prayer with the help of the Holy Scriptures and the guidance of the Holy Spirit. Have you ever asked similar questions?

We've also included personal stories from each woman who are just like you. Scan the QR code for exclusive content to hear how prayer has transformed their lives.

In the second section, I encourage you to challenge yourself: commit to writing out your prayers for 30 days. As you do, listen closely to how the Lord speaks to you. Record His promises, guidance, and the ways He responds.

Grace and peace to you from God our Father and the Lord Jesus Christ,

Shelsea Becker

Table of Contents

"...praying at all times in the Spirit, with all prayer and supplication. To that end, keep alert with all perseverance, making supplication for all the saints."
(Ephesians 6:18)

"Be careful for nothing; but in every thing by prayer and supplication with thanksgiving let your requests be made known unto God. And the peace of God, which passeth all understanding, shall keep your hearts and minds through Christ Jesus."
(Philippians 4:6-7, KJV)

"Rejoice always, pray without ceasing, give thanks in all circumstances; for this is the will of God in Christ Jesus for you." (1 Thessalonians 5:16-18)

What is Prayer?

Prayer is a lifeline to God. For the Christian, it should be as natural as breathing.

Prayer is simply spending time in the presence of God and engaging in authentic, raw, and transparent conversations with the Creator of the universe. These conversations with Jesus can be short or long, depending on your mood or circumstance. They can be loud shouts and angry yells, to quiet sobs or inaudible sighs. The tone, pitch, or decibel level doesn't determine the significance of the conversation.

Your prayer time can be spent during a leisurely drive, watching the sunrise, or sitting on your bed. You can have your eyes closed or open; sitting or standing; kneeling or laying prostrate on the floor. You can dance during your prayer, or you can linger in the stillness. The point is prayer is an exchange between you and God.

Time spent in prayer will strengthen your relationship with Jesus and cultivate a life-giving fellowship. All that matters is that you communicate with God. He can handle your questions, frustration, discomfort, anger, pain, heartache, joy, astonishment, love or whatever else you choose to discuss. He just wants you. Remember that genuine prayer, involves two-way communication–speaking and listening. God communicates, too. Take time to pause and be still, waiting for His response. *~**Apryl Randall***

Prayer is our way of open communication with God. He speaks to us through His Word, and we speak to Him through prayer. It's a two-way conversation!
~ Lexi Levatino

Simply, prayer is communication with our loving Father. The Gr word {*proseuche}* for prayer is used 127 times in the New Testament, and it means submitting our desires, needs and vows toward God. So, let's do just that, without ceasing!
~Thresa Lawson

Prayer is communicating with God. We share our thoughts, feelings, and desires with the Father, through the Son, by the Spirit. When we intentionally focus on being with Him. Prayer brings both God and us unparalleled joy!
~Kelly Levatino

For me, prayer is having a meaningful conversation with Jesus, my Lord and Savior, a friend who loves me unconditionally and always wants the best for me. It is engaging in loving fellowship with God, submitting my will to Him, and resting in the peace of knowing He has every situation under control. It is an act of worship, a time to thank Him for every blessing in my life. It is a sacred and beautiful time with the Holy Spirit that always empowers me and leaves me feeling loved and encouraged.
~Victoria Steelman

Postures of Prayer

Outward posture is not the most important element of prayer, but it should reflect the inside posture of our hearts–humble, surrendered, broken, grateful, loving. With that, the Bible lists 5 specific postures of prayer.

Sitting:
Teachable Spirit, Fellowship, and Intimacy

Standing:
Service–Ministry to God and Others

Kneeling:
Meekness and Surrender

One's face to the ground:
Humility

Hands lifted up:
Mercy, Blessing, Help, Praise

Beyond physical postures, what we do with our voices in prayer is also important. Sometimes the best thing we can do is *be still and know that He is God*, without saying a word (Ps. 46:10). When awed and amazed, one is often in silence. Also, when Hannah prayed in anguish for God to give her a child, *"she was speaking in her heart, only her lips were moving, but her voice was not heard"* (1 Sam. 1:13). No one could hear her silent prayer but God, and He answered.

Sitting
Teachable Spirit–Fellowship–Intimacy

2 Sam 7:18, *"Then King David went in and sat before the Lord and said, 'Who am I, O Lord God, and what is my house that you have brought me thus far?'"*

Judges 20:26, *"Then all the people of Israel, the whole army, went up and came to Bethel and wept. They sat there before the Lord and fasted that day until evening, and offered burnt offerings and peace offerings before the Lord."*

Luke 10:38-42, *"Now as they went on their way, Jesus entered a village. And a woman named Martha welcomed Him into her house. And she had a sister called Mary, who sat at the Lord's feet and listened to His teaching. But Martha was distracted with much serving. And she went up to Him and said, 'Lord, do you not care that my sister has left me to serve alone? Tell her then to help me.' But the Lord answered her, 'Martha, Martha, you are anxious and troubled about many things, but one thing is necessary. Mary has chosen the good portion, which will not be taken away from her.'"*

Luke 22:14-16, *"And when the hour came, He reclined at table, and the apostles with Him. And He said to them, 'I have earnestly desired to eat this Passover with you before I suffer. For I tell you I will not eat it until it is fulfilled in the kingdom of God.'"*

Ephesians 2:4-7, *"But God, being rich in mercy, because of the great love with which He loved us, even when we were dead in our trespasses, made us alive together with Christ—by grace you have been saved— and raised us up with Him and seated us with Him in the heavenly places in Christ Jesus, so that in the coming ages He might show the immeasurable riches of His grace in kindness toward us in Christ Jesus."*

Revelations 3:20, *"Behold, I stand at the door and knock. If anyone hears My voice and opens the door, I will come in to him and eat with him, and he with Me."*

Standing
Service–Ministry to God and Others

Mark 11:25, *"And whenever you stand praying, forgive, if you have anything against anyone, so that your Father also who is in heaven may forgive you your trespasses."*

1 Kings 8:22, *"Then Solomon stood before the altar of the Lord in the presence of all the assembly of Israel and spread out his hands toward heaven."*

2 Chronicles 20:5-6, *"And Jehoshaphat stood in the assembly of Judah and Jerusalem, in the house of the Lord, before the new court, and said, 'O Lord, God of our fathers, are you not God in heaven? You rule over all the kingdoms of the nations. In your hand are power and might, so that none is able to withstand you."*

2 Chronicles 34:31, *"And the king stood in his place and made a covenant before the Lord, to walk after the Lord and to keep His commandments and His testimonies and His statutes, with all his heart and all his soul, to perform the words of the covenant that were written in this book."*

Ephesians 6: 10-15, *"Finally, be strong in the Lord and in the strength of His might. Put on the whole armor of God, that you may be able to stand against the schemes of the devil. For we do not wrestle against flesh and blood, but against the rulers, against the authorities, against the cosmic powers over this present darkness, against the spiritual forces of evil in the heavenly places. Therefore take up the whole armor of God, that you may be able to withstand in the evil day, and having done all, to stand firm. Stand therefore, having fastened on the belt of truth, and having put on the breastplate of righteousness, and, as shoes for your feet, having put on the readiness given by the gospel of peace."*

1 Kings 8:54, *"Now as Solomon finished offering all this prayer and plea to the Lord, he arose from before the altar of the Lord, where he had knelt with hands outstretched toward heaven."*

Kneeling
Meekness and Surrender

Psalm 95:6, *"Oh come, let us worship and bow down; let us kneel before the Lord, our Maker!"*

Chronicles 6:13, *"Solomon had made a bronze platform five cubits long, five cubits wide, and three cubits high, and had set it in the court, and he stood on it. Then he knelt on his knees in the presence of all the assembly of Israel, and spread out his hands toward heaven."*

Daniel 6:10, *"When Daniel knew that the document had been signed, he went to his house where he had windows in his upper chamber open toward Jerusalem. He got down on his knees three times a day and prayed and gave thanks before his God, as he had done previously."*

Luke 22:41, *"And He withdrew from them about a stone's throw, and knelt down and prayed."*

Acts 7:60, *"And falling to his knees he cried out with a loud voice, 'Lord, do not hold this sin against them.' And when he had said this, he fell asleep."*

Acts 20:36, *"And when He had said these things, He knelt down and prayed with them all."*

Ephesians 3:14, *"For this reason I bow my knees before the Father."*

One's Face to the Ground
Humility

1 Kings 18:41-42, *"And Elijah said to Ahab, 'Go up, eat and drink, for there is a sound of the rushing of rain.' So Ahab went up to eat and to drink. And Elijah went up to the top of Mount Carmel. And he bowed himself down on the earth and put his face between his knees."*

Job 1:20-21, *"Then Job arose and tore his robe and shaved his head and fell on the ground and worshiped. And he said, 'Naked I came from my mother's womb, and naked shall I return. The Lord gave, and the Lord has taken away; blessed be the name of the Lord.'"*

Numbers 20:6, *"Then Moses and Aaron went from the presence of the assembly to the entrance of the tent of meeting and fell on their faces. And the glory of the Lord appeared to them."*

Matthew 26:39, *"And going a little farther He fell on His face and prayed, saying, 'My Father, if it be possible, let this cup pass from Me; nevertheless, not as I will, but as You will.'"*

Luke 5:12, *"While He was in one of the cities, there came a man full of leprosy. And when he saw Jesus, he fell on his face and begged him, 'Lord, if you will, you can make me clean.'"*

Revelation 1:17, *"When I saw him, I fell at His feet as though dead. But He laid His right hand on me, saying, 'Fear not, I am the first and the last,'"*

Nehemiah 8:6, *"And Ezra blessed the Lord, the great God, and all the people answered, "Amen, Amen," lifting up their hands. And they bowed their heads and worshiped the Lord with their faces to the ground."*

Hands or Eyes Lifted Up
Mercy–Blessing–Help–Praise

1 Timothy 2:8, *"I desire then that in every place the men should pray, lifting holy hands without anger or quarreling."*

Mark 6:41, *"And taking the five loaves and the two fish, he looked up to heaven and said a blessing and broke the loaves and gave them to the disciples to set before the people. And he divided the two fish among them all."*

John 11:41, *"So they took away the stone. And Jesus lifted up His eyes and said, 'Father, I thank you that you have heard Me.'"*

John 17:1, *"When Jesus had spoken these words, He lifted up His eyes to heaven, and said, "Father, the hour has come; glorify your Son that the Son may glorify you,"*

Psalm 121:1-2, *"I lift up my eyes to the hills. From where does my help come? My help comes from the Lord, who made heaven and earth."*

Psalm 141:2, *"Let my prayer be counted as incense before you, and the lifting up of my hands as the evening sacrifice!"*

Did Jesus Pray?

We know the answer to be "yes," but can you count from memory how many times? I counted 38 times, but the truth is, Jesus' life was full of prayer. This sustained and kept Him united with the Father. Jesus did not pray out of mere obedience, but out of a deep, intimate relationship. He also modeled for us how we should pray daily and without ceasing.

Here are some examples of Jesus praying to the Father:

He blessed food at the meal, giving thanks for it. *"Then Jesus took the loaves, gave thanks to God, and distributed them to the people. Afterward, He did the same with the fish. And they all ate as much as they wanted."* (John 6: 11, NLT)

Peopling can be hard. Jesus needed times of solitude. *"But Jesus often withdrew to the wilderness for prayer."* (Luke 5:16, NLT)

Have you ever needed to make a big decision? So did Jesus! *"Now it came to pass in those days that He went out to the mountain to pray, and continued all night in prayer to God. And when it was day, He called His disciples to Himself; and from them He chose twelve whom He also named apostles."*
(Luke 6: 12-13, NKJV)

In John 17:1-26 (NLT) we see that Jesus prays for Himself, His disciples, and all believers just before His journey to the cross. *"Jesus looked up to heaven and said, 'Father, the hour has come. Glorify your Son so He can give glory back to you. For you have given Him authority over everyone. He gives eternal life to each one you have given Him. And this is the way to have eternal life— to know you, the only true God, and Jesus Christ, the one you sent to earth. I brought glory to you here on earth by completing the work you gave me to do.'"* **~Tammy Manning**

The Lord's Prayer

"Father, hallowed be Your name. Your kingdom come. Give us this day our daily bread, and forgive us our sins, for we ourselves forgive everyone who sins against us. And lead us not into temptation."
(Luke 11:2-4, NIV)

In Jesus' model for how His disciples should pray, He provides five areas of focus:

- God's name is to be honored–the focus on His everlasting glory *("Father, hallowed be Your name")*;
- God's kingdom come–the focus on His eternal will *("Your kingdom come")*;
- God's provision is given–the focus on our present *("Give us each day our daily bread.")*;
- God's forgiveness is granted–the focus on our past *(Forgive us our sins, for we also forgive everyone who sins against us.)*;
- God's deliverance will be provided–the focus on our future. *("And lead us not into temptation.")*

What Does it Mean to Pray in Jesus' Name?

It's interesting that the Bible never actually says word for word "In Jesus' name we pray!" However, it does advocate for doing so. *"Whatever you ask in My name, this I will do, that the Father may be glorified in the Son. If you ask Me anything in My name, I will do it."* (John 14:13-14)

The Apostle John also wrote this, *"...but these (words) are written so that you may believe that Jesus is the Christ, the Son of God, and that by believing you may have life in His name."* (John 20:31). John's whole purpose in writing his account of Jesus' life is so that those who read it may believe that (a) Jesus is who He said He is, and (b) He can save you and give you life. John chose these words to give testimony to Jesus' character and to spur people on to believing in Jesus' power and saving grace.

When we ask something in Jesus' name, we are telling the Lord, "I choose Your path over my own. Please help my desires line up with Your desires for my life." So at the end of a prayer, after you have asked God to reverse the dent on your car or miraculously cook dinner, by saying "In Jesus' name I pray," you are ultimately submitting to His will. With that phrase, we are communicating that even if that bill does not get paid on time, we trust that God's plan is better than our own. We are choosing to walk in His path instead of ours, acknowledging that it is He who holds all the power.

~Lexi Levatino

Who Do We Pray To?
God, Jesus, or the Holy Spirit ?

God is three in One, and each One plays very significant roles in our lives. He is God the Father, God the Son, and God the Holy Spirit. The question then is does it really matter which divine person, or nature, of the Trinity we address pertaining to our need? Absolutely, without a doubt I believe it does! Why else would He reveal Himself to us in very unique and powerful ways in order to meet us at the place we need Him to intervene?

★ God the Son came to be our Savior, Jesus our Lord, our Redeemer, Healer, and Intercessor. He came down from His throne, was conceived by the Holy Spirit, and born of a virgin to be the propitiation of all sin. So we would most assuredly pray to Jesus when we need Him to take our petition and request before the Father. And most certainly when we are praying for salvation. In this, we go before the throne with a repentant heart because we believe Jesus is our Savior and Lord.

★ When bringing our requests to God the Father, we remind Him of His promises to us. When we are in need of healing, restoration, stability and comfort, we pray to the Father, in Jesus Name.

★ The Holy Spirit has been given to us so that we can know who God is and how to follow Him. Often the Holy Spirit will speak to us in our minds by giving us a thought or idea. He is always moving in our lives instructing, correcting, convicting, and guiding us. The Holy Spirit helps us hide the Word deep in our hearts that we do not sin against Him and that we have constant and continuous ammunition to keep the enemy and our flesh under total subjection to Father God. *~Lois Underwood*

Should Prayer be Formal or Informal?

"The prayers of a righteous man are powerful and effective."
(James 5:16, NIV)

At 16, on a missions trip to Guatemala, I witnessed something that changed the way I pray. As we entered the local village, the sky rapidly darkened. We also were aware of fear on the faces of the villagers, so the missionaries gathered us to pray. As we looked around, we saw rain falling heavily around us, but everything inside the circle in the village center stayed dry. I watched in complete amazement as the visibly shaken villagers stepped out from the rain and into the circle to hear what the missionaries were saying.

A young boy stood up and spoke loudly, calling for the missionary's attention. I watched him as he pulled another little boy to his feet. The missionary quietly whispered that the boy had asked them to pray for his cousin who had been deaf and mute from birth. The sermon had been on the healing power of Jesus, and now the entire village was watching to see if our claim had any legitimacy. The missionary let us pray for a few moments. Then he reached out his hand, laid it on the boy's ear, and simply said, "be healed in Jesus' name." His cousin watched wide eyed in amazement as the boy began to shout "Mama! Mama!" Because of this miracle, nearly half that village came to know Jesus.

All of that from the simplest of prayers. No flowery words of prose or poem. No structured recitation or memorized words. Prayers were simply offered up from the depths of a righteous heart. The informality of honest prayer is always the catalyst for closeness with the Lord. It wipes away all pretense and distance, and closes the gap of tradition with the oil of His presence. *~**Christy Catlin***

Should We Pray Out Loud or Silently?

The simple answer is it depends on the situation. One day while on a photo shoot, I felt a pause in my spirit and heard the Lord say, "You are in danger!" I took a deep breath and started to look around me. At that moment, a white sedan with three young men drove up to where we were. They looked at me and my photography gear and then at my clients. My heart started to race. I knew immediately the young men were going to try to rob me and that my young clients could also be in danger.

I began to pray, rebuke the devil, and declare that my clients and I would not be hurt. I also prayed in the Spirit. If I could just stay strong in my faith and hold the line, I knew we would be okay.

I watched as another man got out of his truck and noticed what was happening. He began to march intently toward the car. I knew God had sent him like a guardian angel to help us at that moment. As he approached their car, they sped away. He then turned and entered the building. I assume the man called the police because a police car came racing into the parking lot, asked if we were okay, and then drove around to find the men. That day, I prayed out loud to put the enemy on notice, and I prayed silently without ceasing in the Spirit so as not to alarm my clients.

In 1 Samuel 1:13 (AMP), we read, *"Hannah was speaking in her heart (mind); only her lips were moving, and her voice was not heard, so Eli thought she was drunk."* This is another story of a desperate cry to God for help. If we were to read on, we would find that the Lord heard her cry and answered her silent prayer! So, whether you pray out loud or silently, what's important is that you pray with reverence, respect, and the right heart. Remember, the Lord knows our needs before we even ask Him—and He hears us no matter how loud our voice. **~*Victoria Steelman***

How Long Should Prayer Be?

Interestingly, the Bible doesn't give a simple answer. While long, intense prayer sessions can be powerful, it seems that regular, **consistent**, and **frequent** prayer is what strengthens us. I think of it this way *the treadmill that was set up in my bedroom didn't strengthen me until I used it*–**consistently** *and* **frequently.**

We know that Adam and Eve walked with God in the Garden. Daniel prayed **consistently** three times a day (Daniel 6:10). **Frequently**, Jesus withdrew from people to pray (Mark 1:35, Mt. 14:23). The book of Acts records that the twelve apostles delegated authority to seven chosen men so that they could give their attention to prayer and the ministry of the word (Acts 6:4).

The Bible also couples times of prayer and fasting. And records times when the seriousness of the situation results in prolonged times of heartfelt prayer for a desired outcome. Before His death, Jesus *"prayed more fervently, and He was in such agony of spirit that His sweat fell to the ground like great drops of blood,"* (Luke 22:44, NLT). It's not recorded just how long Jesus prayed that night, but it was long enough to go some distance only to come back to find His disciples sleeping three different times.

The Apostle Paul tells us this, *"be unceasing in prayer"* (1 Thess 5:17, AMP). Another translation says *"pray continually"* (1984 NIV), which can also be described as *"without interruption"* (Concise Oxford English Dictionary). *"Pray constantly"* (New Jerusalem study Bible) and *"Never stop praying."*

So, when you awake in the morning, until you fall asleep; as you go throughout your daily activities, as you drive in traffic; pray without ceasing, continually, without interruption, constantly, and never stop!! *~**Laura Anne Smith***

What Types of Prayers are in the Bible?

Growing up, I struggled to communicate with God effectively. I never fully understood how to have an authentic conversation with Him. When Jesus transformed my life, I realized that prayer was more than a mere list of requests; it was a journey towards a more meaningful relationship with the Creator of the universe. As I've grown, exploring various prayer forms has been eye-opening. Realizing that I can lift my hands to the heavens, or pour out my heart in tears on the bedroom floor, with the certainty that God listens, has been a significant revelation.

Several years ago, my brother stared at me with dead eyes that seemed emptied of hope. He was addicted to a dangerous drug. I spent every day for months interceding and petitioning God to wreck my brother, to influence his choices, to change his heart, to block the addiction, to go to a rehab facility, to remove people from him that were feeding his addiction. I cried out to the Lord in my car, while in the shower, before bed, while on my knees or standing with my hands raised. But my biggest prayer was "Father, reveal yourself to him today. Allow him to see and hear you. Heal his body from the addiction. Purify his mind with Your thoughts. Let him experience You, Father. Let him know your love as I do. Let him accept salvation through You, Jesus. Save him." Sometimes it was quietly spoken, sometimes yelled, and sometimes through inaudible tones because I didn't have the strength to speak. No matter the volume or intensity, God hears!

Today, my brother is living a sober life, and as a chemical counselor guiding other men of all ages who have faced similar struggles! Now, when I think of my brother's life story, my prayers are frequently loud, occasionally off-key, yet always full of joy! All praise and glory belong to our Heavenly Father! What the enemy intended for harm, the Lord cast into the sea! *~Apryl Randall*

The Bible lists at least nine main types of prayer:

- **Prayer of Faith** (<u>James 5:15</u>) *"And the prayer of faith will save the one who is sick, and the Lord will raise him up."*
- **Prayer of Agreement** (<u>Acts 2:42</u>) (also known as corporate prayer), *"And they devoted themselves to the apostles' teaching and the fellowship, to the breaking of bread and the prayers."*
- **Prayer of Request** (also known as petition or supplication), (<u>Philippians 4:6</u>) *"Do not be anxious about anything, but in everything by prayer and supplication with thanksgiving let your requests be made known to God."*
- **Prayer of Thanksgiving** (<u>Psalm 95:2-3</u>) *"Let us come into His presence with thanksgiving; let us make a joyful noise to Him with songs of praise! For the LORD is a great God, and a great King above all gods."*
- **Prayer of Worship** (<u>Acts 13:2-3</u>) *"While they were worshiping the Lord and fasting, the Holy Spirit said, 'Set apart for me Barnabas and Saul for the work to which I have called them.' Then after fasting and praying they laid their hands on them and sent them off."*
- **Prayer of Consecration** (also known as dedication), (<u>Matthew 26:39</u>) *"And going a little farther He fell on His face and prayed, saying, 'My Father, if it be possible, let this cup pass from me; nevertheless, not as I will, but as You will.'"*
- **Prayer of Intercession** (<u>1 Timothy 2:1</u>) *"First of all, then, I urge that supplications, prayers, intercessions, and thanksgivings be made for all people."*
- **Prayer of Imprecation** (<u>Psalms 69</u>)
- **Praying in the Spirit** (<u>1 Corinthians 14:14-15</u>) *"For if I pray in a tongue, my spirit prays but my mind is unfruitful What am I to do? I will pray with my spirit, but I will pray with my mind also; I will sing praise with my spirit, but I will sing with my mind also."*

What Does it Mean to Pray in the Spirit?

Our team comes from various denominational backgrounds, and we have the *utmost* respect for the differences between us because, at the end of the day, we all believe the same core tenets of Christianity and love one another *deeply*. Whatever we believe about the subject, we are unanimous that this is not a make-or-break topic.

Historically, some Christians have interpreted the phrase as praying in tongues. Others have understood it as meaning sometimes praying in accordance with the Holy Spirit (together and/or with the same prayer points in mind) and other times praying with our human spirits, with our whole selves–our heart, soul, mind, and strength.

The phrase "pray in the Spirit" is used, primarily, in three different verses. *"And **pray in the Spirit** on all occasions with all kinds of prayers and requests." (Ephesians 6:18, NIV)* "But you, dear friends, by building yourselves up in your most holy faith and ***praying in the Holy Spirit**, keep yourselves in God's love as you wait for the mercy of our Lord Jesus Christ to bring you to eternal life," (Jude 20-21).* "Well then, what shall I do? I will **pray in the Spirit**, and I will also pray in words I understand." (1 Cor 14:15, NLT).* Interestingly, the NLT is the only version that translates the phrase this way. The ESV and NIV both say, *"pray with my spirit."*

After doing an in-depth study of these scriptures, in my humble opinion, the best way to answer our question is this: pray in our human spirits with the power of the Holy Spirit, in known or unknown languages. And, if you've accepted Jesus as both your Lord (boss) and your Savior (redeemer), you have the Holy Spirit inside of you at all times! Romans 8:11 says the same power that raised Christ from the dead lives in us! Let's pray like it!
~Kelly Levatino

What is an Intercessor?

I learned intercession through spending hours in prayer. I would pray, cry, worship, and talk to God. I found myself many times laid out on the floor, praying what I saw in the spirit realm. When you begin to connect with God on a level of intercession, it pushes you past what is seen with the natural eye and takes you into the heart of our Father. When this happens, what you pray isn't coming from you, but from the Holy Spirit, who makes intercession for us according to Romans 8:26-27 (NKJV), *"Likewise the Spirit also helps in our weaknesses. For we do not know what we should pray for as we ought, but the Spirit Himself makes intercession for us with groanings which cannot be uttered. Now He who searches the hearts knows what the mind of the Spirit is, because He makes intercession for the saints according to the will of God"*

Intercession means going to the throne of Grace (Hebrews 4:16) boldly petitioning our Father for the needs that He has put on our hearts. I always ask God to align my heart with His, to break my heart for what breaks His, and to align my heart to rejoice in what He rejoices. I submit myself to Him every morning, and I crucify my flesh to the obedience of Christ (Galatians 5:24).

It is in our partnership with God as we pray from a right heart, that heaven comes to earth and meets us with the holy incense of God's glory. As we stand in faith for what we do not see (Hebrews 11), God always shows up and has His way. May we get to a place where unbelief is dead, flesh is dead, natural eyes are dead, and the Spirit of Christ is awakened in us. May we be empty of ourselves and filled to the brim of who Christ is in us. This is when God's power can truly flow through us. When an intercessor is at a place where God is welcome to do whatever He wants to do and the fleshly man is dead, what then could God really do?

~Sara Prather

Why Do We Pray?

Prayer, to me, is uplifting. It is asking our Heavenly Father to move, touch, or uplift the desires and concerns of our lives. In prayer, we make a solemn request for help; or an expression of thanks addressing the Only Wise and True God who knows all, sees all, and is ready to answer our requests. We seek Him, not just when we want something from Him, but also in turning from any wickedness–whether in us, or within the generations before us. In prayer, we ask Him for forgiveness of our sins and to cleanse the sins of our forefathers.

We pray to know the heart of the Father and His desire for our lives. Prayer is our communication line to God about our wants, our needs, our hardships, and our questions. It helps us to receive and give forgiveness. Prayer is the way we get involved with God's eternal work. When we pray, we are participating in God's will being accomplished in our lives, and the lives of others. In all of this, prayer is a privilege.

Psalm 33:12 (KJV) says, *"Blessed is the nation whose God is the Lord; And the people whom He hath chosen for His own inheritance."* This encourages us to peacefully and quietly pray according to 1 Timothy 2:1-2 (KJV), *"I exhort therefore, that, first of all, supplications, prayers, intercessions, and giving of thanks, be made for all men; for kings, and for all that are in authority; that we may lead a quiet and peaceable life in all godliness and honesty."*

Ultimately, prayer helps us live out Romans 12:1-2 (KJV), *"I beseech you therefore, brethren, by the mercies of God, that ye present your bodies a living sacrifice, holy, acceptable unto God, which is your reasonable service. And be not conformed to this world: but be ye transformed by the renewing of your mind, that ye may prove what is that good, and acceptable, and perfect, will of God."* My encouragement to you is to be filled with the Holy Spirit and pray in tongues. Worship the Lord and be obedient to His Word. And make your life a life of prayer. *~Louvina Gross*

Can My Prayers Influence Others?

To say that watching my grandmother pray left an indelible impression on my young mind is an understatement. I'll never forget the day my grandma realized I was present as she concluded her prayers. As she slowly began to rise and wipe the tears from her eyes, her face actually glowed. Her eyes glistened with a confident look of total satisfaction. She knew everything would be alright with her loved ones, because she knew, HE heard her prayers. As she walked toward the doorway, she said, "Thresa, how long have you been standing there?" I answered, "Grandma, do you do that all the time?" She cackled, because my grandma never just laughed, she cackled in a wonderful, happy way. She replied, "I do." I asked, "How can you remember all our names and problems?" Again the cackle, "I just do." And, yes she did, til her dying day.

In her final years on earth, Grandma's knees gave out from arthritis and her mobility was limited. She spent much time in her recliner, surrounded by her Bible, notepads, and tape player. People from all over the country would call or visit Grandma for counsel and prayer. After her promotion to heaven, my aunt collected all the pages of notes where Grandma had written down the prayer requests. My aunt kindly sent me some pages from her countless collection of prayer requests written on napkins, notepads, or the back of a bill. It was so beautiful to read of the many times that I had been on a mission trip and Grandma had covered me in prayer. So, to answer the question, "Can our prayers influence others?" The answer is a resounding YES!

~Thresa Lawson

Can Prayer Be Worship?

What is prayer? What is worship? Can prayer be worship? How should we worship? How should we pray? Do you ever feel like all you have is questions?

In our Western church culture, we often forget that "worship" isn't a specific time or act, but a call to surrender our lives. In Jesus' own words He tells us, *"But the hour is coming, and is now here, when the true worshipers will worship the Other in spirit and truth, for the Father is seeking such people to worship Him. God is spirit, and those who worship Him must worship in spirit and truth."* (John 4:23-24, ESV) This means the Father is calling us to Himself and pleading with us to examine and posture our hearts, our minds, and our bodies to one of worship. So what is worship?

With every fiber of my being, I believe the answer is found in Matthew 22:37-38 (ESV), *"You shall love the Lord your God with all your heart and with all your soul and with all your mind. This is the great and first commandment."* I love God with all of my heart! I give him my worship and praise daily! But, if I'm honest, life is sometimes just really hard. At times, I grow weary and frustrated with my prayers. I know that my heart should sit in the safety of *"Thy will be done,"* but the hard things of life, or the weight that we carry for others in prayer is sometimes very heavy. I love that Habakkuk teaches that true worship incudes crying out to the Lord and being honest before Him. He can carry the weight of what I feel and, He will answer; *"Look among the nations, and see; wonder and be astounded. For I am doing a work in your days that you would not believe if told."* (Habakkuk 1:5, ESV)

The root of prayer and worship is always going to be what's authentically in our hearts, and my greatest desire is to have my heart posture always pointed to the Father. *"It is written, 'You shall worship the Lord your God, and Him only shall you serve.'"*
(Luke 4:8, ESV) **~Heather Grissom**

Prayer Journal
30 Days of Meditation

Date:

Scripture Verse:

Date:

Scripture Verse:

Date:

Scripture Verse:

Date:

Scripture Verse:

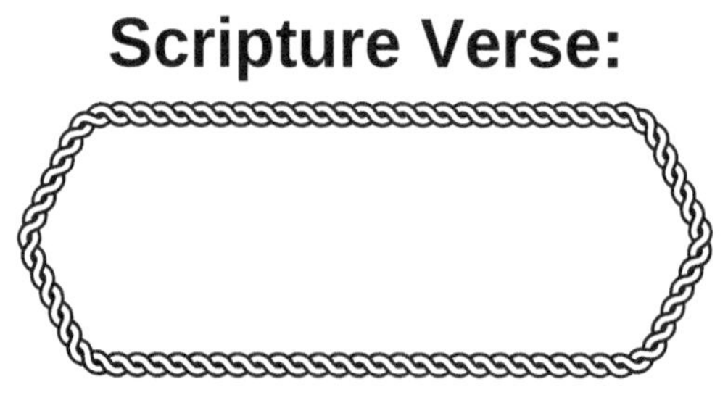

Date:

Scripture Verse:

Date:

Scripture Verse:

Date:

Scripture Verse:

Date:

Scripture Verse:

Date:

Scripture Verse:

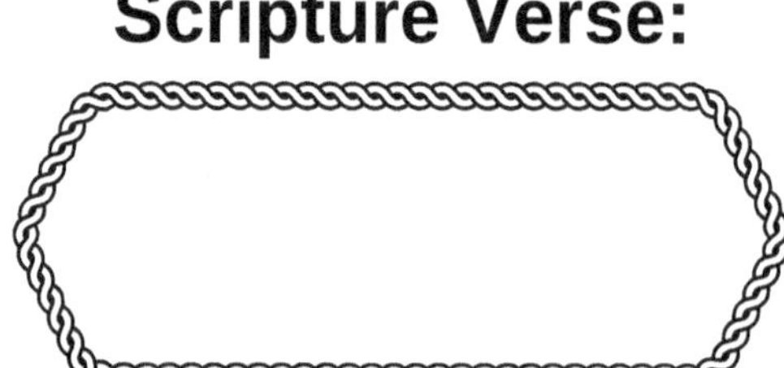

Date:

Scripture Verse:

Date:

Scripture Verse:

Date:

Scripture Verse:

Date:

Scripture Verse:

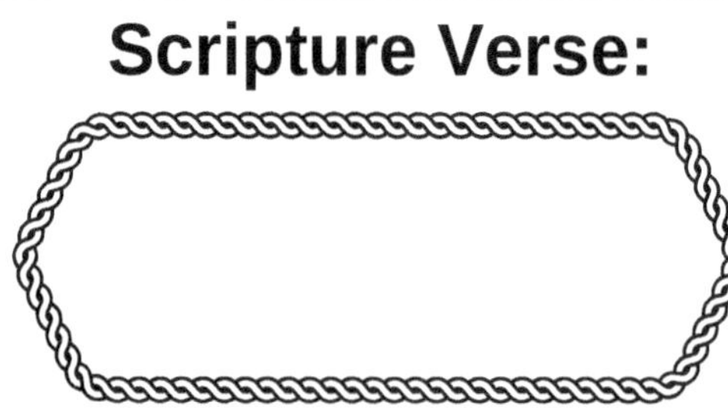

Date:

Scripture Verse:

Date:

Scripture Verse:

Date:

Scripture Verse:

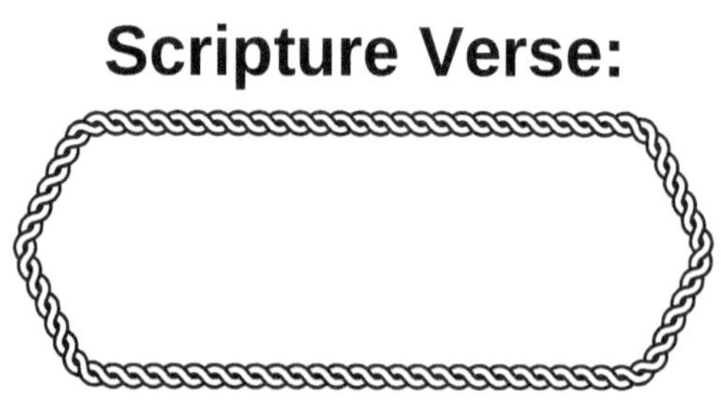

Date:

Scripture Verse:

Date:

Scripture Verse:

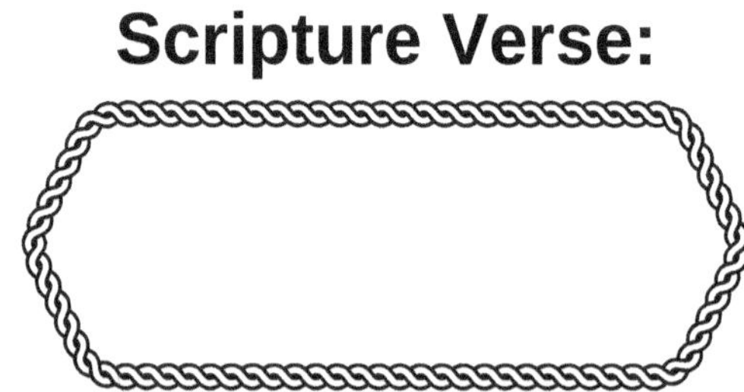

Date:

Scripture Verse:

Date:

Scripture Verse:

Date:

Scripture Verse:

Date:

Scripture Verse:

Date:

Scripture Verse:

Date:

Scripture Verse:

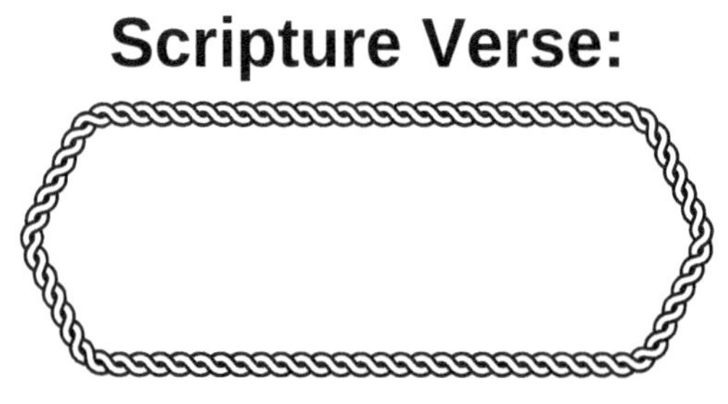

About the Authors

Shelsea Becker

Shelsea is the President of LYN Ministries, INC. and the founder of She Will Conference. She is a speaker, humorist, radio personality and creator of Girl's Weekend God's Way. Her best friend and greatest supporter is her husband, James, and she has two children, Savanna and Bryce. Shelsea enjoys her hot tub, sunrises over the ocean and telling everyone about the love of Jesus.

Tammy Manning

Tammy is one of the She Will Conference Speakers and the National Outreach Director. She is also an encourager and connector. She has served the local church in ministry for 24+ years. Tammy is a wife, mother, grandmother and lover of Jesus and tentmaker for the Kingdom of God.

Lexi Levatino

Lexi is a key partner in managing merchandise and social media posts during the She Will Conference. She is a senior in high school, a competitive varsity cheerleader, and the daughter of Kelly Levatino. Lexi enjoys going to concerts, and her favorite place on earth is Disney.

Lois Underwood

Lois is the North West Quadrant Prayer Leader for the She Will Conference. She is a devoted mother of three and proud grandmother of seven, with seven great-grandchildren. As a born-again believer, she experiences the full redemption of Jesus Christ daily, trusting in His grace, mercy, and Word to guide her. Despite life's challenges, Lois stands firm in her faith, knowing she is equipped by God to live in freedom and blessing.

Christy Catlin

Christy is a She Will Conference Worship Leader. She is also a pastor, worship leader and author and has been serving in ministry with her husband for the last 20 years. They have 4 children that keep their lives full of laughter and chaos. Their life goal is to see the church rise up in Holy Spirit power and experience genuine freedom & unity.

Victoria Steelman

Victoria is one of the She Will Conference Speakers and the National Development Director. As a Christian Country Recording Artist, she was awarded 2024 Christian Voice Magazine's gospel music fan awards Female Horizon Artist of the year and 2024 ICGMA's Female Horizon Vocalist of the year. Victoria is a wife, mother and GMommy to 9 grandchildren.

Laura Anne Smith

Laura Anne serves at the National Registration Director for the She Will Conference. She and her husband have lived for over 30 years in the Nashville, TN area where they homeschooled their sons, and coached Bible memory programs. Laura Anne continues as a homeschool tutor, and will return to school herself in January 2025 to pursue a Master's degree in Biblical and Theological studies. She also combines her passion for teaching and the study of the Bible to create materials and teaching through her company, Know God's Word.

Apryl Randall

Apryl is one of the She Will Conference Speakers, a women's pastor, youth pastor, and co-host of a radio and podcast show. She adores her husband, Jack, and their three daughters, Kylee, Haylee, and Addyson. Apryl adores her husband Jack and their three daughters, Kylee, Haylee, and Addyson. She'll never say no to tacos and she believes coffee is a love language.

Kelly Levatino

Kelly is a Bible teacher, an Observational Comedian, one of the She Will Conference Speakers, and the National Marketing Director. She is a proud wife to Elian and mother to Lexi and Allie. In her free time, Kelly enjoys drinking coffee, watching UGA football and not cooking.

Sara Prather

Sara is one of the She Will Conference Speakers and the National Prayer Director. She is also a prayer intercessor, minister of the Gospel and missionary for Christ. Sara is a wife, mother to three amazing children, mother-in-law to two beautiful women and "Eema" to five grandchildren. She is a student of Christ who strives to serve as the Holy Spirit directs and considers home to be where the Lord sends her.

Louvina Gross

Louvina or as we lovingly call her, LuLu, is the South East Quadrant Prayer Leader for the She Will Conference. She is a retired Veteran with 20 years in the service and taught JROTC for 17 years. She has been transformed from being a victim of verbal, physical, mental, and sexual abuse into a redeemed woman who is blessed to be saved, healed, and delivered by the Blood of the Lamb. With a love for God's Word backed by a Bachelor's in Theology, Louvina is a gap connector for the King, praying for souls.

Heather Grissom

Heather is a She Will Conference Worship Leader as well as being a musician and songwriter. She is a wife of 18 years to her high school sweetheart and has 3 beautiful children. She serves the faithful King in the local church with her husband, who is the pastor. In her free time, Heather loves to travel and do absolutely anything outdoors with her family.

Thresa Lawson

Thresa is one of the She Will Conference Speakers and the National Hello Hard Director. She is a doctoral prepared nurse practitioner and ordained minister and is often described as a fiery bundle of energy. Thresa is the mother of four children and grandmother of fifteen. In her spare time, she enjoys gardening and working on her ranch in Mount Calm, TX, where she lives with her husband.

Books from Past
She Will Conferences

She Will Anchor Deep is a beautiful collection of 52 heartfelt devotions that invite you to experience Jesus more deeply!

Whether you're floating peacefully or being tossed about in a storm, we are all called to anchor deep in the Word of God

"We invite you to embark on a **"Raise Up"** journey through the heartfelt and inspiring personal stories from the women on our SheWill Conference team. As you read through these narratives, we invite you to not only connect with the storytellers but to embark on your own RAISE UP story. Will she Raise Up? She Will!"

HOLD THE LINE
shewill
CONFERENCE